Ci[ty]

impres[sions]

Bristol etchers 1910–1935

SHEENA STODDARD

Published in association with
**City of Bristol
Museum & Art Gallery**
REDCLIFFE
Bristol

First published in 1990 by Redcliffe Press Ltd in association
with the City of Bristol Museum & Art Gallery.

British Library Cataloguing in Publication Data
Stoddard, Sheena
    City impressions : Bristol etchers 1910–1935
    1. English paintings. Special subjects : Avon. Bristol
    I. Title
    758.9942393

    ISBN 1-872971-20-2

Typeset and printed by The Longdunn Press Ltd., Bristol.

CONTENTS

ACKNOWLEDGEMENTS

I would particularly like to thank Celia Barclay for permitting me to use her unpublished account of Nathaniel Sparks, and Guy Woollard for the information he provided about Dorothy Woollard and Reginald Bush. John Broadbelt and Terry Cleeve of the Bristol Savages kindly allowed me access to the records of their society. The index of local artists, compiled by Anthony Beeson and his colleagues at the Avon Central Library, has been invaluable.

No museum publication could ever come to fruition without the help and support of colleagues. Francis Greenacre and Karin Walton read the text and made many helpful suggestions. Andy Cotton took the photographs, Greta Shiner typed the manuscript and Brian Boyd has, over several years, provided much happy discussion about the work of this fine group of Bristol etchers.

SHEENA STODDARD
ASSISTANT CURATOR OF FINE ART, CITY OF BRISTOL MUSEUM & ART GALLERY.

ABBREVIATIONS

ARCA	Associate of the Royal College of Art
ARWA	Associate of the Royal West of England Academy
fl.	flourished
PRE	President of the Royal Society of Painter-Etchers and Engravers
RA	Royal Academy
RE	Royal Society of Painter-Etchers and Engravers
RWA	Royal West of England Academy

INTRODUCTION

From about 1910 until the mid-1930s there were over a dozen artists in Bristol regularly exhibiting etchings of a consistently high standard. Today, when there are again outstanding printmakers working in the city, this first flowering deserves reassessment.

In Britain the etching revival, as it is often called, had gathered pace in the second half of the nineteenth century. It was firmly established by the formation in 1880 of what later became the Royal Society of Painter-Etchers and Engravers (RE). Their title 'Painter-Etchers' distinguished the society's members as artists who were neither illustrators of books nor reproductive engravers and the concept of the original print was firmly established. A print was now regarded as equally worthy a medium for an artist's expression as a watercolour, a drawing or an oil painting. Etching was at the height of its popularity in the first decades of this century and the fashion for collecting prints peaked in the 1920s. The boom years ended with the economic collapse of 1929.

The etchings and other intaglio prints illustrated here have been selected from the permanent collection of the City of Bristol Museum and Art Gallery and augmented with five from a local private collection and two from the Bristol Savages' collection. The definition of what constitutes a 'Bristol etcher' is necessarily flexible; some artists were born in Bristol and learnt their craft at the Municipal Art School under Reginald Bush (1869-1956), others came here to teach or to live for a number of years. Some, such as Nathaniel Sparks (1880-1956) and Dorothy Woollard (1886-1986), moved to London but retained their links with the area until at least the 1920s. Stanley Anderson (1884-1966) and Malcolm Osborne (1880-1963) could not be omitted, for Bristol was where they spent their youth although London was where they achieved success. Their mature work is well-documented elsewhere so only two early Anderson etchings and two of Osborne's superb drypoint portraits are illustrated. Robin Tanner (1904-1988) has been excluded altogether for although he was born in Bristol he moved at an early age to Chippenham and is regarded as a Wiltshire etcher.

Bristol had produced etchers of only minor interest at the end of the nineteenth and beginning of the twentieth century. The most prolific was Charles Bird (1856-1916) who, from the early 1880s, etched monotonous views of Bristol and of architectural subjects throughout the country. He also produced historical pieces with titles such as *Bristol in ye Olden Time*. There were other etchers making similar prints but they have not been included in this survey for they used etching primarily as a means of reproducing a drawing rather than for the potential expressiveness of the medium itself. After the arrival of Reginald Bush in Bristol the standard of etching skills rose dramatically.

Bush came to Bristol in 1895 and for thirty-nine years was Principal of what was to become the Municipal School of Art. He had trained in London at the Royal College of Art (RCA), probably under the great teacher and printmaker Frank Short (1857-1945), and was to achieve some national fame for his etchings of trees. Sir Frank Short (knighted in 1911 during his tenure as President of the Royal Society of Painter-Etchers) was head of the engraving school at the RCA from 1891 to 1924. It was the quality of his teaching, and the discipline which he required of his students, that determined the high technical quality of British etching into the 1930s. A full course under him took five years. Like Short, Bush must have been an inspiring teacher. There were few specialized schools in the country for etching but after Bush had arrived in Bristol he soon established a thriving class. His were the first provincial students to win the British Institute scholarship for an etched portrait study and several won scholarships to study under Short in London. One of them, Malcolm Osborne, was to succeed Short when he retired.

The best-remembered Bristol etchers are those who moved to London to continue their education under Short, were elected Associates and then Fellows of the Royal Society of Painter-Etchers and had their work reproduced in the annual publication *Fine Prints of the Year*. The Fellows of the RE, Anderson, Bush, Osborne, Sparks and Woollard have entries in the pioneering publication on the artists of the etching revival, *British Etchers 1850–1940* by K. Guichard, and their work is represented in national collections. The other etchers featured here are virtually unknown outside Bristol's collection. Some regarded themselves primarily as painters in oil or watercolour, and as printmaking was only one aspect of their work they would have had little aspiration to be elected to the ranks of the RE. With the exception of Frank Skinner (b. 1896, fl. 1915–1931) who did not exhibit in London, all the artists featured here sent work in one medium or another to the Royal Academy. Their names will not be found in the standard reference books on printmakers yet in their time they not only exhibited locally but most contributed to the prestigious American print exhibitions at Chicago and Los Angeles.

The Chicago Society of Etchers was founded in 1910 with only twenty members. When formed, it was the only etching society in the USA, but Chicago was soon followed by other regions. The Print Makers Society of California started in 1914 and held its exhibitions in Los Angeles. By 1930 the Chicago society numbered one hundred and fifty members. Membership was worldwide with members living in Italy, France, Sweden, Germany, England, Canada, Japan, India and China. From the mid-1920s Bristol's etchers contributed to their large annual exhibition held at the Art Institute of Chicago. In 1927 there was a particularly strong Bristol contingent with Bush, his son-in-law Ernest Godding (1894–1931), Gwendoline Cross (c. 1900–1966), Alexander Heaney (1876–1936), Kathleen Jebb (1878–c. 1950), Willis Paige (1890–1960), Frank Skinner and Olive Stephens (c. 1885–1935) all exhibiting from Bristol addresses. Anderson and Osborne, by now fully-established artists, were there along with Woollard who had settled in London. Hilda Hutchings (b. 1890, fl. 1913–1947) exhibited in other years.

The limited edition was a device to limit the availability of an image and thereby increase collectors' demand for it. This was of mutual benefit to the dealer and the artist whose work he promoted. In the first decade of this century the number of collectors increased substantially and prints by sought-after masters were often over-subscribed before they had even been published. This meant that when they later (sometimes immediately) appeared for sale at auction there was great competition for them and ludicrously high sums were paid. The craze for collecting was at its height in the 1920s and for a few years in the middle of that decade some etchings were used as a speculative commodity, like shares. This could not last and prices began to fall before the Wall Street crash of 1929 virtually ended the etching boom. Etchings of quality were still being made but there was no longer a lucrative market for them and by the end of the 1930s many artists had turned to other mediums or were making their living elsewhere, such as in teaching or illustrating.

A handsomely illustrated volume *Fine Prints of the Year* was published every year from 1923 to 1938 and reproduced the work of some two hundred British artists, as well as many foreign ones, during that time. Anderson and Osborne appeared, and were highly praised, in every issue. Bush, Woollard and Sparks were represented with one, two and four prints respectively in the first few issues. A directory listed practising etchers and the prints they had made or published in an edition during the previous year. Artists who did not have a dealer to market their work would probably print only on demand the numbers that they had sold during an exhibition. Inevitably, few prints by Bristol's Alexander Heaney or Willis Paige appear on the market today and the artists themselves are virtually unknown. Both specialised in etching and presumably could have achieved election to the RE, had they so wished, to further publicise their work.

Reviews of *Fine Prints of the Year* in the 1930s show that the annual became a substitute for collectors who could no longer afford to buy the prints themselves during the years of the economic depression. The collapse of the market can be charted from Malcolm Salaman's opening comments in his editorial prefaces where he never doubted that demand would revive. In 1930 he wrote 'The print-markets of Great Britain and America have suffered a partial eclipse during the past year' but this was 'not a sign that public interest in the graphic arts is on the wane, or that genuine collectors are no longer eager to add fine prints to their collections'. In 1931 he reported that etchers and engravers had been as active as ever despite the economic depression and in 1932 that 'our graphic artists have kept up their spirits'. By 1934, 'The great and beautiful art of etching . . . appears now to have fallen temporarily out of favour with the picture-buying public' but he considered it only a passing phase of fashion. By 1937, however, the new editor, Campbell Dodgson, was proclaiming 'All honour to our etchers if they still work so well for love and not for money' and the following year he revealed that 'some of the most distinguished etchers and engravers have suspended their activity in the field of graphic art in favour of the more remunerative practice of painting'. The annual review was never published again.

During the years of the etching revival the Bristol Art Gallery, which had opened in 1905, often purchased prints by national and local artists at the Royal West of England Academy and the Bristol Savages' exhibitions. The Royal West of England Academy's annual exhibitions in Bristol were a showcase for the work of artists throughout the country and not only for those with West Country connections. Short himself exhibited there and artists who had long since left the area, such as Anderson, Osborne and Sparks, showed their work regularly from the early 1920s. The Bristol Savages are a society of artists, exclusively male, which continues to thrive today and work by six of their early members is illustrated here. As today, members had a deep affection for their convivial society. Anderson continued to exhibit at their annual exhibitions for several years after he had left

Bristol, Cyril Skinner (c. 1908-1970) remained a member even though he had moved to Luton to teach and ceased to exhibit with them, while Harry Banks (1869-1947), Bush, Heaney and Paige seem to have shown much of their output there.

Reginald Bush's teaching and the staff he gathered around him at the Municipal School of Art are particularly important. They produced both a high standard of work themselves and imparted a firm knowledge of the art of etching to their students. They were not the *avant garde* but all were good, traditional etchers working in the established styles of the nineteenth-century revival. The demand was for views of local and continental scenes and the artists who were making a living from their art, such as Anderson, Sparks and Woollard, certainly etched 'pot-boilers' at one time or another. Anderson was later to admit it. Woollard is the most under-appreciated of the students who won scholarships under Bush and then moved to London to further their careers. Although her work was admired when she was a student at the RCA and noticed by critics in the 1920s she achieved little more success. Despite this, her etchings are among the finest.

There were of course other artists producing etchings in Bristol during the 'golden years' of the revival but this selection has been based on quality and chosen to show the examples in Bristol's collection. Artists who were highly prolific but whose work was pedestrian, such as Edward Sharland (c. 1888-1967), have been omitted even though their work is very familiar in Bristol today.

During the 1920s, when etching was at the peak of its popularity in this country, the standard of work produced by many Bristol artists was indisputably high. It cannot be claimed that there was a distinctive Bristol school of etching with any marked stylistic coherence, but rather that the thorough teaching of Reginald Bush launched some artists on national careers and that other, lesser artists, were inspired by the quality of work exhibited by him, his colleagues and former pupils.

STANLEY ANDERSON, RA, RE, 1884–1966

Stanley Anderson was born in Bristol but lived most of his working life in London and Oxfordshire, becoming one of the most respected British printmakers of his time. He exhibited widely and internationally, won many awards, is represented in collections throughout the world and, in 1951, received the CBE. Although it would be invidious to omit him from an account of Bristol's etchers, for it was here that he learnt to etch and exhibited his first works, he cannot properly be described as a Bristol artist and only two early works are illustrated.

He was the son of a Bristol engraver whose work included decorating silver salvers and cups with engraved ornament. His father was determined that he should follow the same trade and the reluctant Stanley was apprenticed for seven years. The young man was equally resolved to become an artist and paid for an evening's tuition a week at the Bristol Municipal School of Art studying under Reginald Bush. His first recorded etching was of a Bristol building, St Peter's Hospital, in 1906. Anderson was an artist member of the Bristol Savages from 1907 and exhibited regularly there until 1916.

At the age of twenty-four he discovered that the only way he could leave Bristol to study in London was to win the British Institute's scholarship for an etched portrait. The rules stipulated that he had to do this before his twenty-fifth birthday. He duly concentrated on improving his portrait etching and won the scholarship (of a mere 18/- a week), arriving in London in January 1909 to join Frank Short's etching class at the Royal College of Art. He also studied at Goldsmiths' College, where he was to become a teacher in 1924, but admitted later that he did not much like the atmosphere of art schools and preferred to study at the British Museum or to work in his own room.

Anderson's prime interest was in the human figure but he established his reputation as an etcher of topographical scenes, for that is what sold, and animated the architecture with lively figures. His drypoints of the 1920s, many of them continental scenes, brought him success. From 1929 he concentrated on line-engravings and today his best-known works are engravings depicting rural activities, such as hedging and hurdle-making, which he exhibited from 1933.

[Plate 1]
Bristol Savages Menu 1908
Drypoint with pen and ink

Anderson first exhibited his work at the Bristol Savages in 1908, having been elected the previous year. His father was a lay member of the society. This menu may well show the young artist himself, with a nonchalant pose and flowing scarf. He was known for his thick, dark hair and there are some similarities with Osborne's much later portrait of him (plate 35). It is a charming, fluid drypoint, preserved in a scrapbook along with other Savages' menu cards and cuttings. The mouth-watering menu itself is hand-written.

Anderson etched at least five Bristol views between 1906 and 1908 but very few prints were pulled before he destroyed the plates. The Ashmolean Museum, Oxford, has a comprehensive collection of his work including two of the early Bristol subjects. They are rather coarsely executed and are obviously early experiments in the medium.

[Plate 2]
Bookshop, Clement's Inn, London 1909
Etching

This etching was made during Anderson's first year in London and was included in the 1909 Savages' exhibition. It is printed with a heavy surface tone in a warm, sepia ink and is in marked contrast to the clean-wiped engravings of his mature work. The margins of the print have been trimmed, leaving a 'tab' for the signature, in imitation of James Abbott McNeill Whistler (1834–1903). Anderson explained that this accentuated the richness of the print in contrast to the whiteness of the mount.

He continued to exhibit with the Savages for several years and later showed at the Royal West of England Academy from 1923 to 1947, but the London exhibitions at the Royal Academy and the Royal Society of Painter-Etchers and Engravers were the main outlets for his work.

1. Stanley Anderson: *Bristol Savages Menu.*

2. Stanley Anderson: *Bookshop, Clement's Inn, London.*

12

HARRY BANKS, ARWA, 1869–1947

Harry Banks was born in London, the son of a cabinet maker, and educated at Goldsmiths' College and later in Antwerp. In 1902 he designed the dinner invitation cards for the Coronation of Edward VII and Queen Alexandra. That same year he moved from Chelsea to Thorncombe in Dorset.

His connection with Bristol dates from 1917. His only daughter attended school there and the family lived in a flat in Clifton during term-time for some five or six years. Banks was soon part of Bristol's artistic community; he exhibited with the Bristol Savages and at the Royal West of England Academy and Dorothy Woollard etched a portrait of him (plate 60). Although this peripatetic existence between Dorset and Clifton lasted only a few years, Bristol remained the city where he most regularly exhibited his work and he remained a Savage until 1945. As a painter, his more usual subjects were continental views and Dorset and Somerset landscapes.

He exhibited only three times at the Royal Academy, from 1918 to 1920, and those works were probably oils or watercolours. Although he was considered well-known as a watercolourist, exhibiting in France and the USA, this work is virtually unknown today. Contemporaries remarked on his love of strong colour. Holidays were taken abroad in France, Switzerland and Italy and often financed by selling watercolours 'on the spot'. The rest of the year was spent in the house at Thorncombe either painting or tending the idyllic grounds with his wife. He was a friend of the painter Lucien Pissarro (1863–1944), who from 1940 lived barely a mile away at Hewood. They had known each other from before that date but it is not known where or when they met.

Although Banks regarded himself as a painter he is remembered in Bristol for his fine prints which included local scenes. He always printed his own plates (rather than contracting-out the task to a professional printer) and constantly experimented, pulling a variety of states of each print. Intaglio prints are usually most successful when printed in monochrome but Banks also produced aquatints with a most subtle use of colour.

[Plate 3]
Bristol Docks c. 1920
Etching and drypoint

Most of Banks' etched views of Bristol were made in the early 1920s and the working life of the docks was a favourite subject. This panoramic view looks up the Floating Harbour; the houses of Clifton Wood are on the left and the Cathedral is in the distance. The sheerlegs piercing the skyline were a well-known landmark at the yard of the shipbuilders and repairers, G K Stothert & Son.

The foreground is deeply etched whilst the banks of clouds are in finely-worked drypoint.

[Plate 4]
King Street, Bristol c. 1921
Etching and drypoint

Banks printed in an almost painterly manner. He left films of ink on the plate in the shadow areas, and wiped it clean in others, such as where the early morning light streams between the buildings on the left. The carts, not yet harnessed, are silhouetted against the warehouses. Workmen wait near the Llandoger Trow inn.

The Llandoger Trow now incorporates the three gabled houses nearest the queue of men; the further two houses were destroyed in the blitz. The group remains an impressive example of the seventeenth-century vernacular architecture which was still much in evidence in Bristol before 1940.

[Plate 5]
Discharging Cargo at The Grove, Bristol c. 1922
Etching and drypoint

Banks was middle-aged when he first came to live in Bristol and he seems to have enjoyed the bustle of a port after the peace of rural Dorset. His are the only etchings which regularly show an interest in the life of the quays and the constant loading and unloading of vessels.

In the distance is the spire of St Mary Redcliffe with Redcliffe Parade to the right.

[Plate 6]
Broad Quay c. 1922
Etching

Banks was a meticulous and skilful etcher and it is not always easy to distinguish the techniques he employed. The shadow in the foreground is not aquatint but probably a surface tone achieved by a very careful wiping of the plate. It might also have been accomplished by open-bite, the rest of the plate being stopped-out with varnish before being briefly immersed again in the acid. Another technique to create tone, which Whistler used, is to quickly wash the acid across the bare plate with a brush or feather.

In *Broad Quay* Bristol's city centre is still an active port; the final open section of water was not covered over until the late 1930s. Colston Hall is seen in the distance.

[Plate 7]
Bristol Bridge c. 1922
Etching and drypoint, early state

This etching well demonstrates Banks' skill as a printer. The shafts of light in the foreground, the smoke from the funnel and the light shining through the arches of the bridge are all achieved through a very careful wiping of the plate. Although it resembles aquatint all the variation of tone has been achieved during the inking of the plate; it is unlikely that other impressions would be identical with this one.

14

There is a later state of this plate; the birds were removed and a man sweeping was added. A coarse and rather obtrusive aquatint ground was laid and the resultant print is very different in appearance. It was probably an impression of that later state which Banks exhibited with the Bristol Savages in 1931.

The view is taken from Welsh Back with St Nicholas' Church on the left. The terrace beyond the bridge is the back of Bridge Street which was destroyed in the blitz and ultimately replaced by Castle Park.

[Plate 8]
A Farm near Kilve, Somerset c. 1925
Aquatint

The aquatint ground is coarse-grained and, considering the precision of Banks' linear work, it is a surprisingly broad and free use of the medium. This was not a print to be kept in a collector's portfolio and carefully examined for fine detail but a brooding landscape best framed and viewed from a distance.

Kilve is near the coast of Somerset, mid-way between Burnham-on-Sea and Minehead.

3. Harry Banks: *Bristol Docks.*

4. Harry Banks: *King Street, Bristol.*

5. Harry Banks: *Discharging Cargo at The Grove, Bristol.*

6. Harry Banks: *Broad Quay*.

7. Harry Banks: *Bristol Bridge.*

8. Harry Banks: *A Farm near Kilve, Somerset.*

REGINALD E J BUSH, ARCA, RE, RWA, 1869-1956

Reginald Bush was the head of Bristol's art school for thirty-nine years. Shortly after his arrival in 1895 he instilled new life into the school and the number of pupils began to increase. When he retired in 1934 it was said that the Bristol Municipal School of Art had become one of the best art schools in the country. He certainly inspired a younger generation of etchers and many won prizes in the national competitions of the time. Malcolm Osborne was his most distinguished pupil, becoming Professor of the School of Engraving at the Royal College of Art in 1924 after the retirement of Sir Frank Short.

Bush had been born in Cardiff where his father was the head of the School of Science and Art. His brother, Percy, became a famous Welsh rugby international. Reginald studied at the RCA and in 1893 won a travelling scholarship which enabled him to continue his studies in Paris and Italy. He next taught at the RCA for a year before moving to Bristol to take up the post of Principal of what was then called the Government School of Science and Art.

Bush exhibited worldwide, in Europe, the USA and Japan as well as London. He first showed at the Royal Academy in 1895 and his last exhibited work was at the Royal Society of Painter-Etchers in 1946. In 1929 James Laver, of the Victoria & Albert Museum, described him as one of the 'etchers of trees of the last generation' but, during a long career, his output was rather more varied than that suggests. There were landscapes of Wales, Hampshire and the West Country, France and Switzerland. Later in life, after his retirement, he visited Majorca and Tangier and then roamed further afield to Ceylon. Few of these later works are known today. As a keen fisherman he was presumably able to combine his interests by sketching the trees and riverside views he was later to etch or paint in watercolour.

In the 1920s he painted a series of portraits in oil for the Bristol tobacco company W D & H O Wills. The portraits are competent and sympathetic showing the ordinary men and women who had served the company for forty years.

Bush was an eminent and popular member of the Bristol Savages and made a practice of introducing the most promising of his students to the society. For over thirty years he was a familiar figure at their sketching evenings and there are a couple of caricatures of him drawn by fellow Savages. He was described as 'of somewhat commanding appearance with his imperial type beard and geniality'. In 1950 he was made a life member after he had left Bristol to live in London. Now over eighty years old and widowed, he was cared for there by Dorothy Woollard.

[Plate 9]
Book-plate for the Bristol Savages 1913
Etching

The Bristol Savages were founded in 1904 by a group of artists who had been sketching together informally for ten years. Their title came from a Chairman's rebuke during noisy arguments when trying to choose a name for the society. The first annual exhibition was held in 1905. Bush became an active Savage; he was elected as an Honorary Member in 1906, a full Artist Member in 1911 and served as President in 1929. He designed the club badge, contributed regularly to *Grouse*, a periodical produced during the inter-war years, and his etchings were also used as menu-cards and invitations. This book-plate shows a savage holding his torch up to the muses of poetry, art and music.

Meetings were held at a succession of venues until 1919 when the society contributed handsomely towards the purchase of the Red Lodge, a late sixteenth-century house which is now a branch of the City Museum and Art Gallery. Without the timely intervention of Brother Savage J F Eberle, a lay member, the house would have been sold elsewhere and stripped of its oak panelling and other fitments by antique dealers. The society built its club-house, the Wigwam, in the grounds and moved into it in 1920 with its diverse collection of pictures, furniture and exotic curios.

Wednesday evening meetings are still held to the same pattern as in the early years. A sketching subject is set for the artist members to draw in a couple of hours and then an entertainment of music or poetry follows when the lay members have gathered.

[Plate 10]
Bristol Municipal School of Art, Invitation Card 1913
Etching

The school had opened in 1853 as the Bristol School of Practical Art and used studios at the Fine Arts Academy (later the Royal West of England Academy) in Queen's Road. By the time Bush arrived as Head Master, or Principal, in 1895 it had become known as the Government School of Science and Art; in 1903, when it was taken over by Bristol Corporation, the name changed to the Bristol Municipal School of Art, as on this invitation. After Bush retired in 1934 there were great changes; the school was recognised as a Regional College and in 1936 took the title West of England College of Art. Studio space at Queen's Road was still used until the art school moved to new, purpose-built premises at Bower Ashton in the late 1960s. It is now part of the Bristol Polytechnic.

[Plate 11]
Looking East from Ashton Park c. 1917
Etching

Bush was known as an etcher of trees and he never tired of their intricate forms. Later in life he drew 'flamboyant' trees in Ceylon and olive trees in Majorca. Salaman had written the British section of Holme's *Modern Etchings* in 1913 and said of Bush that he 'looks at trees with a loving pictorial eye and a true appreciation of the way they grow'. In 1929 Laver wrote of his 'delight in the patterns made by interlacing branches'. Many of Bush's pupils produced similar compositions.

Ashton Park lies to the west of Bristol. The suburb of Bedminster can be glimpsed through the trees.

[Plate 12]
Building the University of Bristol 1922
Etching

The Wills Memorial Building, known by everyone as the University Tower, is seen here shrouded in scaffolding. It was begun in 1914 but the First World War delayed construction; King George V performed the opening ceremony in 1925. The completed tower can be seen in Gwendoline Cross' and Nathaniel Sparks' etchings (plates 18 and 49).

Bush changed his mind about the composition of his etching. To the right of the foreground figure can be seen the shadowy remains of another. The artist 'burnished-out' his mistake before etching his revised composition on the newly-polished plate.

[Plate 13]
The Bristol Avon at Sea Mills c. 1927
Etching

The view looks up-river towards Bristol, with Sneyd Park on the skyline. The pencil sketch on which it is based was made many years earlier, in 1918, and drawn from Shirehampton golf course.

[Plate 14]
A Little Girl 1922
Drypoint

This tiny drypoint, reproduced actual size, was made for Queen Mary's Dolls' House at Windsor Castle. Princess Marie Louise, a cousin of King George V and childhood friend of Queen Mary, suggested in 1921 that the architect Sir Edwin Lutyens should design a dolls' house. Queen Mary, who was an avid collector of miniature objects, agreed and the Princess organised the ambitious scheme.

Every tiny object in the house was an exact model and the artists and craftsmen who contributed donated their work. Gertrude Jekyll laid out the garden, the leading artists of the day made miniature paintings and authors wrote stories expressly for the library. The writer E V Lucas helped with the collection of watercolours and prints. Seven hundred artists were asked to contribute and their work was stored in cabinets in the library.

This impression was purchased at the 1925 Bristol Savages' exhibition and was the only proof then available. It is unlikely that any other impressions exist apart from the one at Windsor Castle which is entitled *A little maid* and dated 1922. Olive Stephens and Dorothy Woollard also contributed drypoints and it is possible that Bush recommended them to Lucas.

[Plate 15]
Baby Bunny c. 1929
Drypoint

This charming rabbit is a surprising subject for an artist who is known as an etcher of trees and landscapes. In this country Bush exhibited the print only with the Bristol Savages but he chose to send it to the 1930 Chicago Society of Etchers exhibition.

The 1931 *Fine Prints of the Year* recorded an etching on the same-sized plate called *Mickey Mouse*, in an edition of seventy-five, but it is not known today. Bush exhibited the mouse widely as *Little Mick* and it may have been conceived as a companion print to the rabbit.

[Plate 16]
St Malo 1932
Etching

Bush was in his sixties when he made this delightful etching which is in such contrast with his formal landscapes. The line is delicate and large areas of the plate are left bare, suggesting the expanse of sand and sky in a manner reminiscent of Whistler.

The figures are amusingly observed with a wry sense of humour for the antics northern Europeans always seem obliged to perform on beaches. The woman in the deck-chair is well wrapped-up; this could so easily be the English seaside.

[Plate 17]
The Fish Market, Brixham 1933
Etching

Bush etched this plate in the year before he retired as Principal of the Bristol Municipal School of Art. He had retained his interest in the medium throughout his years of teaching and, rather than restricting himself to ordinary topographical views in his later work as did other Bristol etchers, he expanded his range of subject matter instead.

The fish which dominate the bustling scene cannot be positively identified but are probably a small species of shark. Ray are seen on the quay in the background.

9. Reginald Bush: *Book-plate for the Bristol Savages.*

10. Reginald Bush: *Invitation Card.*

11. Reginald Bush: *Looking East from Ashton Park.*

12. Reginald Bush: *Building the University of Bristol.*

13. Reginald Bush: *The Bristol Avon at Sea Mills.*

30

14 & 15. Reginald Bush: Top, *A Little Girl*. Bottom,
Baby Bunny.

16. Reginald Bush: *St. Malo.*

17. Reginald Bush: *The Fish Market, Brixham.*

GWENDOLINE CROSS c. 1900–1966

Gwendoline Cross was born in Bristol. Her parents opposed her wish to be an artist but as soon as she became of age she enrolled at the Bristol Municipal School of Art. She married a fellow student and, after obtaining her diploma, became a part-time teacher there until 1944.

She first exhibited at the Royal West of England Academy in 1923 but was never elected as an associate member. She stopped exhibiting there in 1935, perhaps because of her involvement with a group of ex-students from the art school who held their own exhibition in the RWA galleries. In 1934 she had been a founding member of this New Bristol Art Club and served as its first President; as she told an *Evening Post* reporter 'We want to waken up art in Bristol – get a fresh outlook'. She probably etched for only a decade from her student days until the early 1930s. Only Bristol subjects, a few of London and a couple of reproduction prints after Velazquez and Van Dyck are recorded. Her etchings have much in common with those of Dorothy Woollard who was some fourteen years her senior.

Soon after the war Gwendoline and her husband, Frederick Whicker, moved to Falmouth in Cornwall. They became members of the St Ives Society of Artists and exhibited regularly with them. Gwendoline Whicker was a member of the Board of Governors of Falmouth School of Art for many years and served as its chairman. She was a versatile artist who painted portraits, flowers and still lifes as well as working in silver and enamel. She also did illustrative work for publications, ranging from flowers to anatomy.

[Plate 18]
The University Tower c. 1926
Etching

The Wills Memorial Building was completed in 1925 and Bristol's new landmark immediately became a popular subject for artists (see also plates 12 and 49). This unusual view looks across the University's roofs towards a corner of Berkeley Square and the trees on Brandon Hill, with Dundry church on the horizon. The artist left much of the foreground parapet bare of etched line to concentrate the viewer's attention on the tower itself.

[Plate 19]
Demerara House, Bristol c. 1926
Etching

In 1851 the *ss Demerara* had broken her back on her maiden voyage down the Avon. The figurehead was erected at Quay Head and removed in 1931 when the buildings were demolished for a road-widening scheme. The wooden figure was given to the Bristol Savages but it was so badly decayed that it could not be saved. All that remains in their care is the spear.

[Plate 20]
Clifton from the Avon c. 1928
Drypoint

This section of the river is at the southern entrance to the Cumberland Basin. The building on the quay is the Dock Master's House and the foreground structure is the grid-iron, used by vessels for hull repairs. Windsor Terrace rises above, and the Clifton Suspension Bridge is in the distance.

Several Bristol subjects by Cross are known only by their titles and remain to be re-discovered. For example, the year before she exhibited this drypoint at the Royal West of England Academy she had shown a *Bristol Docks* which she then sent to the Chicago Society of Etchers in 1928.

18. Gwendoline Cross: *The University Tower.*

19. Gwendoline Cross: *Demerara House, Bristol.*

20. Gwendoline Cross: *Clifton from the Avon.*

HORACE H G DAVIS, ARWA, c. 1914–1944

Horace Davis was educated at the Bristol Municipal School of Art and after qualifying taught for a short time at a school in Nottingham. During the Second World War he was a pilot in the RAF and was killed in 1944 when his plane was shot down into the sea off Aden. He is commemorated on the Alamein Memorial in Egypt.

He exhibited at the Royal West of England Academy from 1932 to 1938 and in 1935 his design was chosen for the cover of the souvenir handbook for the events of Jubilee Week in Bristol. Before the war began he had just started to exhibit in London; one painting was accepted by the Royal Academy in 1939. Few of his etchings are known today and it is unlikely that he produced a great number. He was working when the market for etchings had slumped and he was a generation younger than most of the artists included here. His work has the solid craftsmanship to be expected of a pupil of Reginald Bush and Willis Paige.

[Plate 21]
Queen Elizabeth's Hospital 1934
Etching

Horace Davis probably etched this plate when he was a student at the Bristol Municipal School of Art. It is a strong composition with a dramatic viewpoint of the facade of the school. His monogram, bottom left, is consciously modelled on that of the great German engraver Albrecht Dürer (1471–1528).

The Bristol architect Thomas Foster designed this building set on the flanks of Brandon Hill for the City School in 1843. Its premises had formerly been at the bottom of Christmas Steps.

21. Horace Davis: *Queen Elizabeth's Hospital.*

ALEXANDER J HEANEY 1876–1936

Alexander Heaney came to Bristol as an officer in HM Customs and Excise. It is not known where he was born, although he bore an Irish name and spoke with a slight brogue. In the years 1910–13 he is listed as a student at the Royal West of England Academy, where classes were held for study from the model and from casts. These were presumably evening classes. Heaney was never associated with the RWA again and he is the only etcher discussed here who never exhibited at their annual exhibitions. He was elected to the Bristol Savages in 1915 and was a very active member. He was President in 1923, contributed regularly to *Grouse* and exhibited with them until the year before he died.

He occasionally exhibited at the Royal Academy and once in Chicago but was probably the true, enthusiastic amateur who asked for nothing more than enjoyment from his hobby and the companionship of his society. The Savages' historian records him as: 'Never a robust type, he was tall, lean, clean-shaven and with a thick crop of black hair. The sad expression he wore on his face was due, possibly, to his failing health . . . he was of a shy and retiring nature'. He had to retire from work in the early 1930s because of ill-health. He then devoted himself fully to his hobby, specialising in etching, although he also used pastel and watercolour.

Heaney's work is quite different from that of the other Bristol etchers for he was particularly interested in the human figure. He drew some historical costume-pieces for *Grouse* and there are etchings which illustrate Shakespearean or biblical subjects but his most successful works are vigorous prints of Bristol's life in the 1920s. He drew rapidly and his etched line is coarse; the effect is quite different from the subtle printing of his fellow Savage, Harry Banks. He did not experiment with different techniques but usually restricted himself to pure etching, biting his plates deeply.

[Plate 22]
The Public House 1913
Drypoint

Heaney's first recorded etchings, three Bristol views, were made in 1912. This drypoint from the same period is printed with much more surface tone than his later work.

The Public House is the Palace Hotel which stands at the junction of West Street and Lawford Street in Old Market, Bristol. This flamboyant cornerpiece had been built in 1869. Heaney's drypoint shows a crowd which has gathered outside one evening to watch a parade but his main interest is in the flicker of light and shade over the eccentric facade.

[Plate 23]
The Printer [*self-portrait*] 1919
Etching

In this self-portrait, Heaney is seen inking a plate with a dabber, a mushroom-shaped pad which is used to work the ink into the etched lines of the plate. A smaller dabber could be used to lay the wax ground on which the artist drew his original composition, although by this time a roller would have been a more modern implement to use for both processes. He is working on the jigger, a smooth-surfaced box, of similar height to the heater in the foreground. Plates need to be warmed for both applying the ground and wiping off the ink. Before printing his plate after wiping, Heaney would have briefly warmed it again before passing it through the press shown behind him.

[Plate 24]
The Labour Meeting c. 1920
Etching

In the years after the First World War there was a coalition government of Conservatives and Liberals with Lloyd George as Prime Minister. It was a period of inflation with a boom in wages and spending. In the winter of 1920–21 the prosperity ended abruptly. Wages fell heavily in every industry and unemployment doubled in a few months. There were demonstrations by unemployed men in London and provincial cities including Bristol.

Since 1918, Labour candidates had been steadily successful at by-elections and in the 1922 election, won by the Conservatives, they considerably increased their number of MPs. Heaney's Labour meeting might be taking place on the edge of the Downs, at Clifton.

[Plate 25]
The Tobacco Warehouse c. 1921
Etching

Tobacco products formed an important part of Bristol's economy for many years. Three large and monumental, red-brick bonded warehouses have dominated the entrance to the harbour since they were built between 1906 and 1919; this is probably the interior of one of them.

[Plate 26]
Stapleton Quarry c. 1921
Etching

Heaney lived on the outskirts of Bristol at Fishponds and there were several disused quarries between there and Stapleton. This etching probably depicts one of those shown as water-filled on maps drawn in the 1930s. There were two opposite the southern boundary of Stapleton Hospital (now Manor Park Hospital).

[Plate 27]
The Ubley Bus c. 1922
Etching

Heaney could characterize his figures with a few swift strokes of the needle. He had a keen eye for the posture of people whether at rest or in movement and they were usually the chief interest in his compositions.

Ubley is a village south of Bristol at the foot of the Mendip Hills. The bus started from Prince Street in Bristol and this public house may have been there. The elderly lady was in very old-fashioned dress for the 1920s.

[Plate 28]
The Bristol Royal Infirmary c. 1922
Etching

Charles Holden's great extension to the Bristol Royal Infirmary was built between 1906 and 1911. It is now largely masked by later extensions, a sad fate for what has been described as 'one of the most important buildings in the history of modern architecture' (Andor Gomme in *Bristol, an architectural history*, 1979). The artist's use of the pattern of the tramcar wires serves to accentuate the radical modernity of the architecture.

[Plate 29]
In the Gallery c. 1928
Etching

This is one of Heaney's finest prints and shows the Upper Circle at the Bristol Hippodrome. Walter Sickert (1860–1942) had etched theatre and music-hall scenes and Heaney may well have been inspired by him in the choice of this subject. The only source of light comes from the stage below and there is a vivid sense of its dazzle. Each figure is a distinct individual; some are absorbed by the performance but the attention of many is elsewhere.

[Plate 30]
The Fish Market c. 1929
Etching

Heaney did not use a tonal process, such as aquatint, but wiped his plates selectively to suggest light and shade. Here, the areas caught by the light streaming through the door have been more thoroughly wiped than the shadows where a thin film of ink was left on the metal.

This print is considerably larger than the others illustrated here. One of Whistler's maxims had been that 'the large plate is an abomination' and there was much discussion by writers on etching in the 1920s regarding the merits of the vast plates made by Frank Brangwyn (1867–1956). These are far larger than Heaney's but James Laver's comments of 1929 could equally apply to some of that Bristol etcher's works:

> It is a legitimate question what use the huge etchings of Brangwyn can be put to. They are too large to keep in a portfolio; nothing is to be gained by holding them in the hand, for there is no delicacy of workmanship to be seen by looking at them closely. They are obviously intended to be hung upon a wall, and if etchings are to be used as wall-

decorations, perhaps Brangwyn's are the best that could be found for the purpose. But it is wise to hang them not on a staircase, as most etchings should be hung, but in a large room, or at the end of a gallery.

Heaney had depicted Bristol's fish market on at least two other occasions. One painting or print was shown at the Royal Academy in 1914 and another etching at the Bristol Savages in 1924.

22. Alexander Heaney: *The Public House.*

23. Alexander Heaney: *The Printer* [*self portrait*].

24. Alexander Heaney: *The Labour Meeting.*

25. Alexander Heaney: *The Tobacco Warehouse*.

26. Alexander Heaney: *Stapleton Quarry.*

27. Alexander Heaney: *The Ubley Bus.*

28. Alexander Heaney: *The Bristol Royal Infirmary.*

29. Alexander Heaney: *In the Gallery.*

30. Alexander Heaney: *The Fish Market.*

HILDA E HUTCHINGS, RWA, b. 1890, fl. 1913–1947

Hilda Hutchings was born in Grantham in 1890. She studied at the Bristol Municipal School of Art where she subsequently became a teacher. She moved to London in 1925 or 1926 and taught at the West Ham School of Art. Very little is known of her later life but she continued to exhibit at the Royal West of England Academy until 1947 although living in the London area. She was a member of the Print Makers Society of California and exhibited with the Chicago Society of Etchers. She also worked in oil and watercolour and exhibited at the Royal Academy.

  Most of her known etchings are of Bristol subjects. Some of her prints can be rather sparse, leaving areas of the paper bare of etched lines with the plate rather too cleanly wiped.

[Plate 31]
Victoria Cottages, Prewett Street 1914
Etching

This print may date from Hilda Hutchings' student days when she was experimenting with different techniques. It was printed with a heavy surface tone: a film of ink was left on the surface and not wiped away as in her later plates. Her etched line is hesitant compared with the flowing draughtsmanship of Dorothy Woollard.

  The choice of subject is unusual, as few artists chose to depict the alleyways of Bristol's less salubrious areas. This is one of the many courtyards near St Mary Redcliffe where housing was dense and many dwellings had no outlook except for a communal yard. A Board of Trade enquiry in 1908 had found that living conditions in this parish were still in the slum category. By then, the more prosperous people were living in the leafy suburbs and commuting into central Bristol. Redcliffe was one of the areas to be severely blitzed in 1940.

31. Hilda Hutchings: *Victoria Cottages, Prewett Street.*

KATHLEEN M JEBB, ARWA, 1878–c. 1950

Kathleen Jebb was born in Liverpool but lived in Westbury Road, Bristol from 1903 to 1950. At one time, probably in the 1910s or 1920s, she worked as an assistant evening teacher at the Municipal School of Art. It is not known when she died but she stopped exhibiting at the Royal West of England Academy in 1950, having shown her work there for nearly half a century since 1903. She exhibited several times at the Royal Academy from 1914 to 1928, the period which probably coincides with her best work, and also exhibited in her home town of Liverpool. Her work was chiefly in monochrome – etching and drawing – but she also painted in watercolour. Her subjects were the landscape of the West Country and Wales and she does not seem to have ventured abroad. The two prints here are the only examples of her work in Bristol's collection.

There is a paucity of biographical information on Bristol's female etchers for they could not become members of the Bristol Savages and therefore do not appear in the records of that society.

[Plate 32]
Study of an Oak c. 1917
Etching

Trees were a common subject for those familiar with the work of Reginald Bush but Kathleen Jebb was more concerned with showing a bold silhouette than the interlacing of branches. The expanse of water in the distance may well be the Severn estuary.

[Plate 33]
The Severn at Old Passage c. 1925
Drypoint

This is an impeccably printed impression. The blacks of the rich burr of the drypoint are heightened by the wiping of the river area to suggest the sparkle of the water. The print has a marvellous sense of space and moist air in a windswept landscape.

Kathleen Jebb listed this drypoint as one of her principal works in the 1934 edition of *Who's Who in Art*. Another etching of the river, *The Distant Severn*, represented her work at the 1927 Chicago exhibition which included so many Bristol etchers. That print has not been identified today although it might be *Study of an Oak* (plate 32) exhibited under a different name.

32. Kathleen Jebb: *Study of an Oak.*

33. Kathleen Jebb: *The Severn at Old Passage.*

MALCOLM OSBORNE, ARCA, PRE, RA, RWA, 1880-1963

Malcolm Osborne was born in Frome in Somerset, where his father was a schoolmaster, and educated at the Merchant Venturers' School in Bristol. Stanley Anderson, nearly four years his junior, was a fellow pupil. He next studied under Bush at Bristol's art school, became a friend of Nathaniel Sparks and won a scholarship to the Royal College of Art. At this time he was not an etcher but went to London to train as a sculptor. He soon transferred to the Architectural School where he remained for a year before finding his true vocation and learning to etch under Frank Short. There is no evidence that he had already been taught etching by Bush in Bristol. His first recorded print was made in 1904 and he exhibited widely until his death. He succeeded Short as Professor of the School of Engraving at the RCA in 1924 and was awarded the CBE in 1948.

His career was based in London and he did not return to Bristol. Although he initially had to accept tedious commissions for etched reproductions of paintings, the public's growing interest in etching meant that he could turn to the more congenial market for British and continental landscapes and architectural views. It is, however, his drypoint portraits which are his finest work and those of his contemporaries Anderson and Sparks are illustrated here. In their youth their careers had followed an identical and familiar pattern of training in Bristol under Bush and then settling in London.

[Plate 34]
Portrait of Nathaniel Sparks 1921
Drypoint

Sparks and Osborne had been close friends since studying together at Bristol in the late 1890s. In London before the First World War they used to spend their Saturday evenings playing bridge in Sparks' lodgings with another etcher, Alfred Bentley (1879-1923) who had also trained in Bristol. Sparks was a vulnerable man, scruffy and sensitive about his self-perceived ugliness, and Osborne's drypoint is a sympathetic study of the character of his old friend.

Sadly, shortly after the print was made, Sparks and Osborne quarrelled irrevocably over a teaching post. Bentley taught and, after his death in 1923 (as a result of being gassed during the war), the impoverished Sparks hoped for his job. Osborne had some influence in the matter but would not recommend him. The reason was never fully explained but he may have felt that his friend was unsuitable because of his appearance and that he would have been mocked by the students. Sparks refused to see Osborne again or accept his apologies and the friendship of some twenty-five years was never renewed.

[Plate 35]
Portrait of Stanley Anderson, RE c. 1925
Drypoint

Osborne's portraiture was highly regarded by his contemporaries: 'We have few masterly portrait-engravers, but one of them is indisputably Mr Malcolm Osborne' wrote Salaman in 1926 in *Fine Prints of the Year*. He could command good prices for his drypoints which were consistently more expensive than Anderson's or Sparks' work in the RE exhibitions of the 1920s. When this marvellously rich impression was purchased at the Royal West of England Academy in 1925 it cost six guineas, a considerable sum at that time. The size of the edition was probably fifty prints, the same as his portrait of Sparks (plate 34).

Anderson was by now a teacher at Goldsmiths' College and, as he had learnt his craft with the outstanding teachers, Bush in Bristol and Short in London, he in turn taught an etcher of the next generation. Robin Tanner vividly described him in *The Etcher's Craft*:

> Stanley Anderson, an outstanding engraver and etcher, and a consummate master of his craft, was my teacher. He was a spare, cool, taciturn man, so admirably disciplined himself that he countenanced only the highest standards from others in his workshop. No detail of the craft passed him by, and he shared his knowledge with us as a medieval craftsman might have done with his apprentices. He would move silently among us in his indigo smock, his fine strong hands always at work. Step by step each one of us followed his directions, and there was no escape.

34. Malcolm Osborne: *Portrait of Nathaniel Sparks.*

35. Malcolm Osborne: *Portrait of Stanley Anderson.*

E WILLIS PAIGE, RWA, 1890-1960

Willis Paige came to Bristol to become Assistant Principal, under Reginald Bush, at the Municipal School of Art. It is not known where he was born or educated. He is first listed in Bristol street directories in the early 1920s and started exhibiting at the Royal West of England Academy in 1925. He taught at the art school until his retirement in 1950 but it was said that he was bitterly disappointed not to take over from Bush as Principal in 1934. In his own work he specialised in etching and showed a fastidious control of the medium.

He is one of the most under-appreciated of Bristol's etchers. His work was not widely known outside Bristol at the time for although he regularly exhibited locally he rarely showed his work in London. Five etchings were at the Royal Academy between 1932 and 1937, and he had previously shown at Chicago, but he does not appear to have wished to join Bush as an RE. His topographical views included, apart from his local scenes, Dover, Richmond in Yorkshire, and Whitby. On the continent he visited Belgium, the Netherlands and France. After his retirement from teaching he also seems to have retired from practising art. Although he remained a Savage until his death he last exhibited there in 1949 and at the RWA in the following year.

Paige was a popular member of the Savages and was their President three times. Their historian recorded that he was:

> Of somewhat commanding appearance, with his goatee beard and a most charming and courteous manner, he was quickly distinguishable in any company. As someone who liked a drink, with his ready wit and jolly face, he soon fitted into the Tribe . . . He was excellent as a speaker who could hold his audience almost spell-bound . . . Any of his speeches would prove a highlight of the evening, serious or humorous.

He contributed regularly to *Grouse* and was a skilled designer. He is remembered by those whom he taught commercial art as a supreme draughtsman and calligrapher who could draw a perfect ellipse freehand.

[Plate 36]
The Lock, Feeder Road c. 1926
Etching and drypoint

This is one of Paige's finest prints, perfectly capturing the gloomy mood of a rainy day. The composition has an almost claustrophobic intensity with very little of the plate left unworked. It is also printed with noticeably more surface tone than his other work.

The Totterdown Lock was filled-in during the Second World War to reduce the risk of Bristol's Floating Harbour being drained when the city was bombed. The bridge carries the Feeder Road.

[Plate 37]
Dover Harbour c. 1927
Etching

Paige exhibited drawings and etchings of Dover at the 1927 and 1928 Bristol Savages' exhibitions. This print, although competent and carefully drawn, has none of the dramatic intensity of *The Lock, Feeder Road* (plate 36) which he had shown the previous year.

[Plate 38]
The Fancier's Shop c. 1929
Etching

This delicately etched plate is superbly printed. Heavy inking would have masked the fine detail of the baskets and cages and to leave a surface tone, used to such atmospheric effect by Nathaniel Sparks, would have been inappropriate. The artist has therefore wiped his plate thoroughly and the fine network of lines invites close inspection.

The Fancier's Shop, known to everyone as 'Wart Eger's' was on the Horsefair in Bristol. It was not just a pet shop but sold livestock, such as chickens, as well.

[Plate 39]
Chez le marchand de vin c. 1931
Etching

The location of this French or Belgian town is not recorded. Here the artist was much concerned with the minutiae of surface texture, ranging from the crumbling facade of the wine merchant's premises to the washing hanging out to dry across the side street.

Brittany was a popular holiday destination for Bristol artists, easily reached from Plymouth. Paige was a full-time teacher and did not have to rely on selling his prints but Anderson was to complain in later life that he was forced abroad to search for 'foreign subjects' from the mid-1920s, because there was very little market for anything else.

[Plate 40]
Boulby Bank, Whitby c. 1932
Etching

Paige exhibited five etchings of Whitby at the 1933 Bristol Savages' exhibition and he had presumably visited the town not long before. In *Boulby Bank* foreground detail is omitted and attention is concentrated on the housing crowded against the steep bank. The subject demanded meticulous draughtsmanship and the artist was fascinated by the complex of shadows cast by the balcony railings onto the outside staircases.

[Plate 41]
The Merchants' Hall, Bristol 1933
Etching

As in *Boulby Bank* (plate 40) Paige delighted in the strong side-light and the patterns of the cast shadows. His figures, however, are sometimes a little stiff and do not successfully animate the scene.

The Merchants' Hall was built for the Society of Merchant Venturers in 1719-21 but this facade had been almost entirely renewed at the end of the eighteenth century. It stood on the corner of Marsh Street and King Street and is here seen from Thunderbolt Street, now the thoroughfare between the City Centre and Queen Square. The Hall was destroyed in the blitz.

[Plate 42]
La Lieutenance, Honfleur c. 1934
Etching

Paige usually clean-wiped his plates to show the fine detail. All of the tone is achieved by the variation of the density of his hatching or the depth of his bitten line.

There were two main approaches to the printing of an etching plate, either the 'visitor's card' and clean-wiped approach or a selectively-wiped plate with a heavy use of surface tone. A clean-wiped print is easier to pull and many artists do have their editions printed by professional printers to release themselves from the onerous task. The artist who leaves more ink on some areas of the plate than on others, or uses inks of different density or colour on the same plate, is working in a more personal and almost painterly fashion which demands that he does all his own printing. Some contemporary writers criticised such techniques for masking the purity of the etched line and preferred the clean-wiped plates of an artist such as Paige.

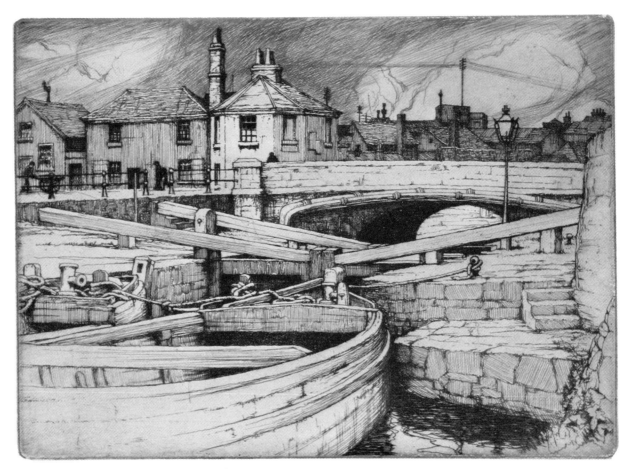

36. Willis Paige: *The Lock, Feeder Road.*

37. Willis Paige: *Dover Harbour.*

38. Willis Paige: *The Fancier's Shop.*

39. Willis Paige: *Chez le marchand de vin.*

40. Willis Paige: *Boulby Bank, Whitby.*

41. Willis Paige: *The Merchants' Hall, Bristol.*

42. Willis Paige: *La Lieutenance, Honfleur.*

CYRIL L SKINNER, ARWA, c. 1908–1970

Cyril Skinner studied at the Bristol Municipal School of Art and gained a British Institute scholarship for engraving in 1928. He joined the Bristol Savages in 1930 and in the following year became an ARWA; at that time he was the youngest artist ever elected. In 1935 or 1936 he left Bristol to join the staff at the Luton School of Art where he became headmaster in 1946. In 1970, four days before he was due to retire, he died suddenly during a visit to relatives in Bristol.

He maintained his membership of the Bristol Savages until 1965 although he had stopped exhibiting there after 1939. He was always enthusiastic about amateur artists and for many years was a member of the judging panel of the Annual Luton Exhibition. It is likely that his teaching duties absorbed his energies and that, after the 1930s, he did not exhibit outside Luton. He had only shown once at the Royal Academy and once in Chicago.

His subjects were local and continental scenes, landscapes, flowers and still lifes. Little of his work is known today. He has no connection with Frank Skinner.

[Plate 43]
Restoration of Bristol Cathedral c. 1931
Drypoint

Cyril Skinner had obviously shown great early promise and, like so many of the students trained by Bush and Paige, he may well have achieved his finest work in his early etchings. Like Heaney, he here shows the working life of the city but the architecture is given as much attention as the figures. It is, however, an almost anonymous architecture and it is only the black silhouettes of the gargoyles which remind us that the men are working on a great Gothic building.

43. Cyril Skinner: *Restoration of Bristol Cathedral.*

FRANK SKINNER, ARWA, b. 1896, fl. 1915–1931

Frank Skinner was born in Bristol, the son of a master coach builder. He studied at the Bristol Municipal School of Art and in 1915 won a British Institute etching scholarship. It is not known whether he was prevented from taking up the scholarship because of the outbreak of war. He first exhibited at the Royal West of England Academy in 1915 but next showed in 1918 when he was serving with the Royal Engineers in France; he sent French subjects.

In 1923 he was appointed to a part-time post of Recognised Teacher of Drawing at the University of Bristol. There was no art department and he may have been a teacher of technical drawing and perhaps in a scientific department. Little else is known about him. He later resigned from his job but the date is not recorded. He last exhibited at the RWA in 1931 but is listed in Bristol street directories until 1939.

He was not a member of the Bristol Savages and did not exhibit at the Royal Academy. Instead of seeking election to the Royal Society of Painter-Etchers he inexplicably chose to join the Chicago Society of Etchers. He sent his work to their exhibitions from at least 1925 to 1929 and was the only one of the etchers living in Bristol who actually joined that society (Anderson and Osborne joined later in the 1920s). Very few of his etchings are known today and neither are his oils or watercolours. They were predominantly landscapes. He has no connection with Cyril Skinner.

[Plate 44]
Silver Severn c. 1923
Aquatint and mezzotint

Aquatint and mezzotint are an unusual combination of techniques. Both are tonal processes; in the sky Skinner laid a mezzotint ground but for the wooded area in the foreground he chose aquatint. This rich impression, depicting the sweep of rain clouds across the edge of the Severn, achieves its effect by the meticulous use of the two processes. It is surprising that so little of the artist's work is known considering the high quality of this print.

44. Frank Skinner: *Silver Severn.*

NATHANIEL SPARKS, ARCA, RE, 1880–1956

Nathaniel Sparks was born in Bristol in 1880, the second son of a violin restorer. The novelist Thomas Hardy was his cousin but there was much acrimony between the families. He was educated at home by his mother before winning a scholarship to the Bristol art school where Reginald Bush taught him to etch. In 1900 he left Bristol to take up another scholarship, at the Royal College of Art, under Frank Short. From his early student days he was a friend of Malcolm Osborne who later made a sensitive portrait of him (plate 34).

Shortly after Sparks' arrival in London the elderly Whistler chose him to print his plates including many of the Venice etchings. Whistler would have accepted only a top class technician and such exacting work was an ideal training for a young printmaker. Sparks settled in Battersea, exhibited at the Royal Society of Painter-Etchers from 1905 and at the Royal Academy from 1906. His career initially showed great promise and at the RA in 1915 Queen Mary bought his *Westminster Abbey seen through the water fountain*. In 1914 his friends Osborne and Bentley had joined the armed forces but Sparks failed his medical examination and spent the war years doing precision work in a munitions factory.

After the war he found it difficult to resume his career successfully. There were other problems. He came down from London to Bristol to nurse his dying father in 1922. The following year Bentley died and then his long friendship with Osborne ended. This must have compounded the problem of his personality; he was shy, sensitive and excessively self-conscious of his ugliness and the size of his nose. Despite praise from Salaman in *Fine Prints of the Year* and the illustration of his work from 1923 to 1925 he increasingly had to turn to landscape watercolours to make a living.

Although he had settled in London and produced a long series of etchings of the city he retained a deep affection for the West Country. In the summers of the 1920s and the early 1930s he toured England and Scotland on sketching tours. He did not travel abroad and therefore could not etch popular continental scenes. Unlike those of Anderson and Osborne his career did not survive the collapse in the etching market. At the 1934 RA and RE exhibitions none of his work was sold. In 1938 he sold his press and left London to care for his aged cousin Katharine Hardy, the novelist's sister. He then lived at various addresses in Somerset and Hampshire before dying in Somerton, Somerset in 1956.

Sparks' work is usually regarded as uneven in quality. His subject matter was broad and it is this very variety, together with some dull topographical 'pot-boilers' which have given him this reputation. However, at his best his prints can stand with the finest work of the 1920s. The Bristol subjects from those years have a particular strength which is often missing from his etchings of other parts of the country.

[Plate 45]
The Dutch House 1910
Drypoint

Sparks' earliest etchings of Bristol, printed when he was a student at the turn of the century, are not known today. When this drypoint was made he had been in London for a decade and the slightly ponderous quality of its line suggests that it may have been based on a much earlier sketch.

The Dutch House stood at the corner of Wine Street and High Street in the heart of Bristol. It was a late seventeenth-century timber-framed building and was one of Bristol's many architectural losses from bombing during the Second World War. The name came from an unlikely tradition that the two facades had been imported from Holland.

[Plate 46]
Cheddar c. 1920
Drypoint

This rapidly executed drypoint is one of Sparks' finest prints and wonderfully suggests rain sweeping across the Mendip Hills. Its warm brown ink is ideally suited to the subject and there is careful use of surface tone to create the lowering sky. Drypoint wears quickly and it is important to obtain an early 'pull' of the print to enjoy the full richness of the medium.

The print does not seem to have been exhibited but stylistically it dates from the early 1920s. At that time he made several fluent drypoints of the English countryside which are among his best work.

[Plate 47]
Melk: a Bristol Character 1924
Etching, modern impression printed by Peter Ford, 1989.

This was the Bristol milkman whose cry was, presumably, 'Melk'. As an old man Sparks was to record his Bristol childhood and the noise of the street life in a busy city. This somewhat comical yet sympathetic image may have been drawn from early memories. Original impressions of this etching are rare as few were printed by the artist. It was presumably not a very saleable image and is unusual in his *oeuvre*. This modern impression was pulled from the plate which is in the collection of the Bristol Art Gallery. The plate was inked to produce an effect as close as possible to Sparks' own style of printing. The lines are very deeply etched and the plate is difficult to print because of the large amount of pressure needed to force the paper into the lines to pick up the ink.

[Plate 48]
Chatterton's Church, St Mary Redcliffe, Bristol c. 1925
Drypoint

Sparks published this print in an edition of fifty, the upper limit for proofs pulled from a drypoint plate. This is an excellent, and therefore probably early, impression. Even in reproduction the velvety blacks of the 'burr' of the medium can be appreciated.

Chatterton was the eighteenth-century boy-poet who forged 'medieval' poetry on old vellum and pretended that he had discovered it in the muniment room of St Mary Redcliffe.

[Plate 49]
The University Tower 1926
Etching

Sparks was one of the many artists inspired by Bristol's newly-built University Tower (see also plates 12 and 18). Here he emphasises its immensity. The cars and pedestrians are dwarfed and the building's dominating position at the top of Park Street is stressed. This is the dramatic effect, the tower as a focal point at the top of the hill, which Sir George Oatley, the architect, envisaged for his building.

[Plate 50]
Portrait of a Man [*self-portrait*] 1929
Drypoint

This is a self-portrait although Sparks exhibited it as *Portrait of a Man*. It perfectly expresses the inner melancholy of this sad and strange figure dressed in shabby clothes. The delicate, silvery tones of his face are strongly in contrast with the bulky folds of the coat. His clasped hands and isolation in an undefined space reveal his crippling self-consciousness even in a self-portrait.

There is an earlier state of the print which is an etched outline. The copper plate was steel-faced (that is a thin coating of steel was deposited by electrolysis on the finished plate) probably before printing the entire edition. This prevents the copper from wearing and the quality of the proofs deteriorating. Sir Frank Short was a well-known exponent of steel-facing but there is evidence that the process can on occasion weaken the impression from a drypoint.

45. Nathaniel Sparks: *The Dutch House.*

46. Nathaniel Sparks: *Cheddar*.

47. Nathaniel Sparks: *Melk: a Bristol Character.*

48. Nathaniel Sparks: *Chatterton's Church, St Mary Redcliffe.*

83

49. Nathaniel Sparks: *The University Tower.*

50. Nathaniel Sparks: *Portrait of a Man* [*self-portrait*].

OLIVE B STEPHENS, ARWA, c. 1885–1935

Olive Stephens was the daughter of a corn merchant and seems to have spent most of her life in Bristol. She was educated at Redland High School, Bristol and then at the Municipal Art School where she was presumably taught by Reginald Bush. She continued her education at the Central School of Arts and Crafts in London where she won a number of prizes. She must then have returned home, as she exhibited from a Bristol address at the Royal West of England Academy from 1908 to 1934. She died in the summer of 1935 at the age of fifty.

In common with her contemporaries her work had been shown at Los Angeles and Chicago but she exhibited at the Royal Academy only in 1913–14 and 1918. She taught etching, printed other artists' editions and provided a drypoint landscape for the Queen's Dolls' House (see caption for plate 14). She also painted landscapes in watercolour but they do not seem to have been particularly distinguished. In her etched work she particularly enjoyed depicting the sinuous forms of trees in blustery weather.

[Plate 51]
Evening on Henbury Golf Links 1913
Etching

This is a typical Olive Stephens motif of trees on the outskirts of Bristol. She was not an exceptional artist but in prints such as this she was clearly influenced by the work of Reginald Bush. Her skill here was in conveying the movement of branches and sky on a windy day.

[Plate 52]
Victoria Rooms, Clifton c. 1926
Etching

Although the perspective of the car is faulty, the detail of the figures has an attractive lightness of touch in the children playing at the fountain and the two elegant ladies strolling towards the viewer.

51. Olive Stephens: *Evening on Henbury Golf Links.*

52. Olive Stephens: *Victoria Rooms, Clifton.*

DOROTHY E G WOOLLARD, RWA, RE, 1886–1986

Dorothy Woollard was one of the most distinguished of the group of printmakers who studied or taught at the Bristol Municipal School of Art. She was born in Bristol and educated at home. During her mid-teens she spent a year or two in France where she did some painting and drawing. By 1908 she was probably at Bristol's art school learning to etch under Reginald Bush. They were to remain close friends until his death. By 1914 she had moved to London, having taken up a scholarship under Sir Frank Short at the Royal College of Art. After the First World War, which she spent drawing maps for the Admiralty, she returned to Bristol before moving permanently to London in late 1921 or early 1922.

Although she had little money during those first years in London and was grateful for commissions from Bristol (see plate 64) her career did seem to be progressing. She exhibited at the Royal Society of Painter-Etchers where Salaman presumably noticed her work. He illustrated two of her stipple-engraved portraits in the 1924 and 1925 *Fine Prints of the Year* and wrote 'Miss Dorothy Woollard is expert with all the methods of the copperplate, and, as far as I know, she is the only artist who has ventured to revive the once popular, but long disused, process of stipple-engraving. And what a charmingly accomplished example is this engaging [portrait of] Mary . . .' Her expertise in so many of the methods of intaglio printmaking echoes the technical mastery of her teacher Sir Frank Short. In the mid-1920s she exhibited at the Royal Academy two reproduction mezzotints after portraits by Reynolds and Lawrence. These laborious prints must have been made on the request of publishers because her original work did not sell sufficiently well. Her pencil drawings were also published in six of Black's *Artists' Sketch Books* series and were sometimes repeated as etchings.

Her subjects included views in northern France and Belgium and the tiny etching she made for Queen Mary's Dolls' House (see caption for plate 14) was a version of a full-sized plate of a picturesque house in Dinan. However, most of her work was of British scenes. In 1929 James Laver wrote that 'She has a summary, vigorous style, and has produced some attractive plates of river-shipping and landscape'. The best of her work has a spontaneity and fluent use of the etching needle combined with a strong sense of design but there are some admittedly dull views, particularly those dating from the years after she had left Bristol. She continued to exhibit at the RE until 1939 and at the RWA until 1947 but the later work is not known. She did work in watercolour, with a loose and harmonious style, but was primarily a printmaker. During the Second World War she worked as a censor; her career as an artist was virtually at an end. After the war, when she was in her sixties, she began translating medical books into braille. In 1950 Reginald Bush moved to London from Bristol to share her Judd Street flat and she nursed him until his death in 1956. In 1972 she moved from London to Cambridge and died there in a nursing home at the age of one hundred years. She was clearly much-loved in her last years but was reticent about her years as an artist and her new friends at the end of her life learned little about her work.

[Plate 53]
A Tortoise 1908
Etching

This charming tortoise must be a student work. The artist's first recorded topographical work, of Bristol Cathedral's cloisters, dates from the following year and is much coarser in comparison. She first exhibited in Bristol in 1910 at the Fine Arts Academy (later re-named the Royal West of England Academy) and her skills advanced rapidly.

Later in life she returned to animal subjects but in a different medium. There was a colour linocut *Pelicans* at the 1927 RWA, and woodcuts *Parrots* and *Cat* at the 1933 and 1935 RE exhibitions.

[Plate 54]
Westbury Church 1912
Etching

This print was issued in 1913 in an edition of sixty impressions by the Bristol dealers and publishers, Frost & Reed. It was one of six views of Bristol including *The Mill on the Harbour* (plate 55). The plates were then destroyed, demonstrating the exclusiveness of the image to collectors. Some contemporary writers on prints strongly criticised the concept of the limited edition as it was not related to the life of the plate. In a letter to Dorothy Woollard in 1924 Herbert Bolton, Director of the Bristol Museum and Art Gallery, wrote of an unspecified print that 'It seems a very pleasing picture, but what a wicked thing to destroy the plate', and soundly censured the publishers responsible.

Both *Westbury Church* and *The Mill on the Harbour* were illustrated, along with three more of her etchings, in the March 1914 issue of the national art periodical *The Studio*. She was then studying under Sir Frank Short in London and was twenty-eight years old, presumably much older than most of her fellow students.

[Plate 55]
The Mill on the Harbour 1913
Etching

This was one of the Bristol etchings issued by Frost & Reed in 1913 in editions of sixty impressions (see plate 54). It is considerably more fluent in style than the *Westbury Church* of the previous year.

It is a view from Redcliffe Wharf with the buildings known as Buchanan's Warehouse. They were formerly part of a granary. The grain was fed by conveyor from the building with the chimney (now demolished) into the adjoining mill. Today, the mill buildings have been converted into flats. In the distance, from left to right, are the city churches of All Saints', Christ Church, St Nicholas' and St Mary-le-Port. Between them are the tall chimneys of Fry's Chocolate Factory in the Pithay area which have also since been demolished.

[Plate 56]
Temple Back c. 1915
Etching and drypoint

This print was also published by Frost & Reed, in an edition of sixty-six, and they still had some in stock in 1939. It is hardly surprising that the edition did not sell; these run-down backs were not a picturesque subject that would appeal to the publishers' usual customers. It is one of the artist's most powerful Bristol plates.

The tone in the foreground is not aquatint but a very controlled use of 'foul-biting'. Foul-biting is usually a mistake, caused when the acid has crept beneath the ground and bitten where it was not wanted. Its effects have, however, sometimes been used creatively by artists.

The view is taken from near the point where Temple Way now sweeps across the Floating Harbour at Temple Bridge. The railway bridge in the distance is at the eastern entrance to Temple Meads Station. On the left, behind the smoking chimney, one of Powell & Ricketts' glass cones at the junction of Avon Street and Cheese Lane can be seen.

[Plate 57]
Burnham Beeches c. 1915
Etching and drypoint

This is a splendid image of the huge, pollarded beech trees at Burnham Beeches, the forest in Buckinghamshire just a few miles north of Slough. The pigs foraging in the foreground are etched more lightly than the massive trunks beyond and the eye is led rapidly into the composition. The artist was based in London at this time. Frost & Reed again published the print, in an edition of sixty; by 1925 they described it as 'scarce'.

[Plate 58]
Pig Market 1917
Soft-ground etching

This market town has not yet been identified. During the years of the First World War Dorothy Woollard exhibited prints of King's Lynn, Yarmouth, Arundel and Hampton Court as well as of Bristol and views along the Thames.

Soft-ground had been popular in England at the end of the eighteenth century as a way of reproducing drawings. It was little used when *Pig Market* was drawn. Sir Frank Short insisted that his students should be complete masters of their craft and they had to learn every intaglio process. Dorothy Woollard's proficiency in so many methods reflects the training she received at the RCA.

[Plate 59]
On the Avon 1918
Drypoint

This tranquil river scene is executed in pure drypoint. It may have been derived from a sketch but it is as likely to have been made on the spot with the artist working from the river bank, a copper plate and needle in her hand instead of a sketchbook and pencil.

[Plate 60]
An Etcher [Harry Banks] c. 1918
Drypoint

Harry Banks (whose work is illustrated in plates 3–8) is here drawing intently onto the dark surface of the grounded plate. The most common instrument used for this 'needling' was made by jamming a steel needle into a wooden holder and fixing it there with sealing wax. Banks had the ability to draw in reverse directly onto the plate; most artists would set up an arrangement with a mirror to reverse their original drawing. As well as having to visualise the composition backwards the artist also has to work from negative to positive, that is the light lines he makes on the dark plate will be the dark lines on the finished print. Diffused lighting of the work surface is essential to avoid the exposed copper glittering too much.

[Plate 61]
In the Arcade c. 1920
Drypoint

Although this print is not dated the pencil sketch for it was published in the book *Bristol: A Sketch Book by Dorothy E G Woollard* in 1920. The ladies' costume is certainly early-1920s and Rowe's music seller's business had changed hands by 1922. Next door, the gentleman with the pipe is scrutinising the stock of Hardy's antique and furniture shop. On the table beside him is a knife grinder. This section of the arcade, then the Lower Arcade, still exists within Broadmead.

A drypoint needle can be difficult to control as it skates across the surface of a plate. Also, every stroke of the tool inscribes the metal and mistakes are time-consuming to remove. Dorothy Woollard drew with particular assurance in this demanding medium.

[Plate 62]
Tower Bridge c. 1920
Etching

The pencil study for this etching was illustrated in a book published in 1920 entitled *Riverside London*, one of Black's *Artists' Sketch Books* series.

The etching was illustrated along with the artist's *Clock Tower, Hampton Court* in the 1923 Print Society Publication *66 Etchings*. The Print Society brought artists and collectors together by worldwide circulation of portfolios of work so that the customer could choose an etching in his own home. The society also organised exhibitions, including a travelling one in the USA where there was a good market for etchings. Dorothy Woollard also exhibited at the Chicago exhibitions, 1927–1929, sending mainly French views.

Tower Bridge is a dramatic composition with an unusual viewpoint of the congested bridge but the etched line lacks the assurance of much of the artist's best work. She had prints made of it by professional printers, writing to Herbert Bolton 'it is rather a tricky plate to pull myself'.

[Plate 63]
Pen-y-Fan c. 1924
Aquatint

This is a pure aquatint without any underlying etching. It is similar to the work of Harry Banks who also had a masterly control of the medium.

Pen-y-Fan is the highest point of the Brecon Beacons in South Wales. A mountain scene was an unusual subject for Dorothy Woollard but she succeeded in conveying the rapid movement of light and shade across the hills.

[Plate 64]
Book-plate for the Bristol Museum & Art Gallery 1922
Etching

In late 1921 or early 1922 Dorothy Woollard had moved to London. She was clearly short of money and the Director of the Museum and Art Gallery, Herbert Bolton, helped by purchasing an etching or two for the collection and by small commissions. She drew fossil insects and investigated the colours of the Egyptian statues in the British Museum for him, as well as designing this book-plate. It was reproduced and used as the institution's official book-plate for many years.

53. Dorothy Woollard: *A Tortoise.*

54. Dorothy Woollard: *Westbury Church.*

55. Dorothy Woollard: *The Mill on the Harbour*.

56. Dorothy Woollard: *Temple Back.*

57. Dorothy Woollard: *Burnham Beeches.*

58. Dorothy Woollard: *Pig Market.*

59. Dorothy Woollard: *On the Avon.*

60. Dorothy Woollard: *An Etcher* [*Harry Banks*].

61. Dorothy Woollard: *In the Arcade.*

62. Dorothy Woollard: *Tower Bridge.*

63. Dorothy Woollard: *Pen-y-Fan.*

64. Dorothy Woollard: *Book-plate for the Bristol Museum & Art Gallery.*

OTHER ETCHERS ALSO WORKING IN BRISTOL
1910-1935

This list does not claim to be complete but concentrates on artists who either exhibited regularly or who are represented in the City of Bristol Museum and Art Gallery's collection. It does not include artists who etched views of Bristol but were simply visitors and had no other connection with the city.

CHARLES B BIRD, ARE, 1856-1916

A most prolific etcher whose undistinguished prints of Bristol are often seen today. At one time he was employed as a designer by Mardon, Son & Hall, the large Bristol printing and packaging company, but he moved to London about 1890. His prints date from the early 1880s until 1915 and were often published by Frost & Reed. He etched numerous topographical and historical scenes of Bristol as well as architectural views throughout the country. They were usually printed with a brown ink. He also made mezzotint reproductions of oil paintings for a London publisher.

FREDERICK E BOLT, 1868-1935

Fred Bolt was an active member of the Bristol Savages from 1909 but rarely exhibited at the RWA. He worked mainly in pen and ink or watercolour. His few prints of Bristol streets are technically poor. Far better are the delightful menus and invitation cards he etched for the Bristol Savages which are preserved in their scrapbooks.

FLORA BUSH, ARWA, fl. 1901-1937

Flora Bush, née Hyland, was born in Kent and studied at the RCA. She married Reginald Bush and taught at the Bristol Municipal School of Art. Although she was chiefly a painter of flowers in watercolour she also produced some etched work.

STANLEY C EADES, ARWA fl. 1910-1938

Eades was an etcher of architectural subjects, particularly churches. His first recorded etching was made in 1910. Apart from a year or two spent in London during the early 1920s he lived in Bristol, where Frost & Reed published his work.

NORAH A FRY, ARWA fl. 1907-1936

Miss Fry may well have been a student at Bristol's art school. By 1919 she had moved to Huddersfield and later, in the mid-1930s, she was living in Llandrindod Wells. She did some work as an illustrator; her known etched work, perhaps from her student days, is coarse.

ERNEST F J GODDING, 1894-1931

Godding was born in Bristol and worked as a designer for the packaging company Mardon,

Son & Hall. He was the son-in-law of Reginald and Flora Bush and a member of the Bristol Savages. He specialised in etching and drawing.

HILDA E JEFFERIES, fl. 1908–1940

Hilda Jefferies was a sister of Kathleen (see below) and etched Bristol subjects until she moved away from the city about 1917. She continued to exhibit paintings and etchings under her married name of Bonsey.

KATHERINE G JEFFERIES, b. 1886 fl. 1908–1964

This artist was born in Bristol where she is known as Kathleen Jefferies. She was a sister of Hilda (see above) and was educated locally before going to the Slade School. She taught music and had moved to London permanently by the early 1920s. She signed her paintings with her married name of Hartnell and her etchings with her maiden name. The etchings date mainly from her early career in Bristol where Frost & Reed published her topographical scenes.

SAMUEL J LOXTON, RWA, 1856–1922

Loxton was by profession an architectural draughtsman and surveyor. He is best known for the many pen and ink drawings of Bristol made for local newspapers at the beginning of the century. He also published etchings of 'old' Bristol. The bulk of these were made between 1899 and 1905 but in 1910 he produced three drypoints of the Avon which are of markedly higher quality. Of these, the *Suspension Bridge* is his most successful print.

EDWARD W SHARLAND, c. 1888–1967

Sharland was a prolific and competent etcher who was apparently never influenced by the outstanding printmakers who were working in Bristol at the same time. He was born in Bristol and apprenticed to follow his father's trade of cabinet-making. He worked for a time as a carver, decorating the furniture for a joinery company in Bitton, but he later seems to have earned his living as an artist. He also painted in oils and was said to be self-taught; his work is rather dull. Topographical etchings of Bristol by Sharland are recorded from 1909. He experimented with colour etching and Frost & Reed published much of his work in the 1920s and 1930s, including a set of four prints of the University Tower. After living in Portishead for some years he later moved to Cornwall where he died in 1967.

WALTER M SKEENS, 1886–1969

Skeens was born in Portsmouth but taught art in Bristol for many years, first at South Bristol School and later at Cotham Grammar School. He regularly showed views of 'old' Bristol at the Bristol Savages and the RWA. He worked in various mediums and did not specialise in etching.

WILLIAM B TAPP, ARWA fl. 1923–1951

Tapp exhibited local subjects at the RWA from 1923 to 1951. He lived in Bristol throughout this period.

INEZ TOPHAM, ARWA fl. 1906–1926

Miss Topham was a pupil of Reginald Bush at Bristol's art school and in 1907 was the first provincial student to win the British Institute scholarship for etching. Her work is unknown today. From about 1920 she lived in London.

L DOROTHY WILMOT, fl. 1908–1934

The artist exhibited from 1917 under her married name of Greenwood; she was then living in Somerset. She later moved to Bristol. Her known etchings of Bristol subjects are crude in technique and date from 1908 to 1911 when she was probably a student.

LIST OF PLATES

Unless otherwise stated all prints are in the collection of the City of Bristol Museum and Art Gallery. Measurements are of the plate mark, height before width. The titles are, in most cases, those under which the prints were first exhibited.

The date of a print has often been determined from its date of exhibition. Thus, if it was shown at the 1925 Bristol Savages' exhibition (held in February and March from 1920 but previously at the end of the year) the date is given as c. 1924. RE exhibitions were also held in early spring, those at the RWA opened in October or November. Abbreviations used for exhibitions where impressions are known to have been included are: BS (Bristol Savages), C (Chicago Society of Etchers), RA (Royal Academy), RE (Royal Society of Painter-Etchers and Engravers), RWA (Royal West of England Academy).

STANLEY ANDERSON, RA, RE, 1884-1966

[1] **Bristol Savages Menu** 1908
Drypoint with pen and ink
186mm × 133mm
By courtesy of Bristol Savages

[2] **Bookshop, Clement's Inn, London** 1909
Etching
230mm × 160mm
K5228
BS 1909

HARRY BANKS, ARWA, 1869-1947

[3] **Bristol Docks** c. 1920
Etching and drypoint
199mm × 315mm
M4158
RWA 1920, BS 1921

[4] **King Street, Bristol** c. 1921
Etching and drypoint
161mm × 200mm
Private collection, Bristol.
BS 1922

[5] **Discharging Cargo at The Grove, Bristol** c. 1922
Etching and drypoint
155mm × 147mm
K5131
BS 1923

[6] Broad Quay c. 1922
Etching
154mm × 145mm
M4306
BS 1923

[7] Bristol Bridge c. 1922
Etching and drypoint, early state
199mm × 235mm
M4308
BS 1923

[8] A Farm near Kilve, Somerset c. 1925
Aquatint
225mm × 308mm
M4612
BS 1926

REGINALD E J BUSH, ARCA, RE, RWA, 1869–1956

[9] Book-plate for the Bristol Savages 1913
Etching
106mm × 81mm
Mb 1907

[10] Bristol Municipal School of Art, Invitation Card 1913
Etching
149mm × 100mm
Private collection, Bristol

[11] Looking East from Ashton Park c. 1917
Etching
252mm × 303mm
M3969
BS 1917, RA, RE, RWA 1918

[12] Building the University of Bristol 1922
Etching
220mm × 163mm
M4309
BS, RE 1923

[13] The Bristol Avon at Sea Mills c. 1927
Etching
265mm × 212mm
M4964
BS, RE 1928

[14] A Little Girl 1922
Drypoint
37mm × 25mm
M4466
BS 1925

[15] Baby Bunny c. 1929
Drypoint
108mm × 100mm
Mb575
BS, C 1930

[16] St Malo 1932
Etching
148mm × 226mm
Mb1104
BS 1932

[17] The Fish Market, Brixham 1933
Etching
201mm × 299mm
Mb1529
BS, RE 1933

GWENDOLINE CROSS, c. 1900-1966

[18] The University Tower c. 1926
Etching
326mm × 220mm
K5166
RWA 1926

[19] Demerara House, Bristol c. 1926
Etching
217mm × 165mm
K5001
RWA 1926

[20] Clifton from the Avon c. 1928
Drypoint
188mm × 265mm
Mb216
RWA 1928

HORACE H G DAVIS, ARWA, c. 1914-1944

[21] Queen Elizabeth's Hospital 1934
Etching
213mm × 214mm
Mb2146
RWA 1934

ALEXANDER J HEANEY, 1876-1936

[22] The Public House 1913
Drypoint
302mm × 225mm
M3973
BS 1917

[23] The Printer [self-portrait] 1919
Etching
206mm × 249mm
By courtesy of Bristol Savages
BS 1920

[24] The Labour Meeting c. 1920
Etching
202mm × 285mm
M4159
BS 1921

[25] The Tobacco Warehouse c. 1921
Etching
246mm × 176mm
M4172
BS, RA 1922

[26] Stapleton Quarry c. 1921
Etching
199mm × 264mm
M4171
BS, RA 1922

[27] The Ubley Bus c. 1922
Etching
200mm × 265mm
M4312
BS 1923

[28] The Bristol Royal Infirmary c. 1922
Etching
162mm × 245mm
M4310
BS 1923

[29] In the Gallery c. 1928
Etching
233mm × 328mm
Mb408
BS 1929

[30] The Fish Market c. 1929
Etching
302mm × 406mm
Mb567
BS 1930

HILDA E HUTCHINGS, RWA, b. 1890 fl. 1913-1947

[31] Victoria Cottages, Prewett Street 1914
Etching
200mm × 139mm
M5058

KATHLEEN M JEBB, ARWA, 1878-c. 1950

[32] Study of an Oak c. 1917
Etching
227mm × 303mm
M3978
RWA 1917

[33] The Severn at Old Passage c. 1925
Drypoint
249mm × 376mm
M4603
RWA 1925

MALCOLM OSBORNE, ARCA, PRE, RA, RWA, 1880-1963

[34] Portrait of Nathaniel Sparks 1921
Drypoint
237mm × 208mm
K5380
RA, RWA 1921, C 1927

[35] Portrait of Stanley Anderson, RE c. 1925
Drypoint
285mm × 235mm
M4600
RA, RWA 1925, RE 1926

E WILLIS PAIGE, RWA, 1890-1960

[36] The Lock, Feeder Road c. 1926
Etching and drypoint
124mm × 174mm
M4644
BS 1927

[37] Dover Harbour c. 1927
Etching
175mm × 250mm
M4958
RWA 1927, BS, C 1928

[38] The Fancier's Shop c. 1929
Etching
190mm × 174mm
Mb573
BS, C, RWA 1930

[39] Chez le marchand de vin c. 1931
Etching
183mm × 175mm
Mb1103
BS, RA 1932

[40] Boulby Bank, Whitby c. 1932
Etching
248mm × 162mm
Private collection, Bristol
BS, RA 1933

[41] The Merchants' Hall, Bristol 1933
Etching
226mm × 352mm
Mb1657
BS 1934

[42] La Lieutenance, Honfleur c. 1934
Etching
243mm × 293mm
Private collection, Bristol
RA 1934, BS 1935

CYRIL L SKINNER, ARWA, c. 1908-1970

[43] Restoration of Bristol Cathedral c. 1931
Drypoint
219mm × 273mm
Mb1106
BS 1932, ?RWA 1933

FRANK SKINNER, ARWA, b. 1896 fl. 1915-31

[44] Silver Severn c. 1923
Aquatint and mezzotint
174mm × 212mm
M4332
RWA 1923

NATHANIEL SPARKS, ARCA, RE, 1880-1956

[45] The Dutch House 1910
Drypoint
229mm × 205mm
K5332
RE 1911

[46] Cheddar c. 1920
Drypoint
200mm × 191mm
K5329

[47] Melk: a Bristol Character 1924
Etching, modern impression printed by Peter Ford, 1989
141mm × 139mm
K5382
RE 1924

[48] Chatterton's Church, St Mary Redcliffe, Bristol c. 1925
Drypoint
362mm × 198mm
K5367
RE 1926

[49] The University Tower 1926
Etching
329mm × 228mm
K5346
RWA 1926

[50] Portrait of a Man [self-portrait] 1929
Drypoint
225mm × 192mm
Mb563
RA, RWA 1929

OLIVE B STEPHENS, ARWA, c. 1885-1935

[51] Evening on Henbury Golf Links 1913
Etching
322mm × 164mm
Mb2170
?RWA 1913

[52] Victoria Rooms, Clifton c. 1926
Etching
157mm × 245mm
Mb2171
RWA 1926

DOROTHY E G WOOLLARD, RWA, RE, 1886–1986

[53] A Tortoise 1908
Etching
65mm × 95mm
M4994

[54] Westbury Church 1912
Etching
125mm × 150mm
Private collection, Bristol
?RWA 1913

[55] The Mill on the Harbour 1913
Etching
257mm × 112mm
M4998

[56] Temple Back c. 1915
Etching and drypoint
193mm × 289mm
M5028

[57] Burnham Beeches c. 1915
Etching and drypoint
250mm × 227mm
M4981
RWA 1915, RE 1916

[58] Pig Market 1917
Soft-ground etching
236mm × 342mm
M5003
RWA 1917

[59] On the Avon 1918
Drypoint
150mm × 226mm
M5010

[60] An Etcher [Harry Banks] c. 1918
Drypoint
154mm × 204mm
M4974
RA 1918, ?RE 1922

[61] In the Arcade c. 1920
Drypoint
234mm × 200mm
M4996

[62] Tower Bridge c. 1920
Etching
250mm × 237mm
M4170
RE, RWA 1921

[63] Pen-y-Fan c. 1924
Aquatint
155mm × 236mm
M5016
RWA 1924, RE 1925

[64] Book-plate for the Bristol Museum & Art Gallery 1922
Etching
125mm × 72mm
M4983

116

GLOSSARY

AQUATINT

Etching is a linear process but aquatint allows the artist to create tones. A fine resin dust is fused to the plate with heat before immersion in the acid bath. The acid bites into the metal around each grain of dust. Graduated tones are achieved by painting the areas which are required to print lightest with a stopping-out varnish. The plate is bitten as many times as necessary for the number of tones required, with the artist stopping-out more of the image between each immersion. The darkest areas of a print are those where the corresponding area of the plate has spent the longest time in the acid.

DRYPOINT

Drypoint is the technique of inscribing directly into the plate with a needle. Scoring deeply produces a 'burr' where the metal is thrown up on either side of the line as in a ploughed furrow. This burr holds the ink and produces a characteristic soft, rich black line. The burr wears quickly and may last for only twenty or thirty impressions. If a plate is worn, or if an artist has scraped away the burr, it can be virtually impossible to tell the difference between an etching and a drypoint. Drypoint is often used in conjunction with other processes and to strengthen the dark areas of etchings to avoid having to re-bite the plate. A drypoint needle can be the same steel point as used for 'needling' a grounded etching plate but a jewel point was also used. A jewel, ideally a diamond point, can be moved much more freely over the surface of the plate and does not throw up so much burr. The fine network of freely drawn lines in Harry Banks' skies may well have been drawn with a diamond point.

ETCHING

The essential principle of etching is that the line is created in the metal plate by the action of acid. The artist first coats his blank plate, usually copper or zinc although other metals are used, with a ground that is impervious to acid. He draws his design with a needle through this ground, exposing the metal. The whole plate is immersed in an acid bath until the lines are sufficiently bitten. The biting may only occur once but if lines of different depth are required the plate is removed from the acid after the lightest lines have been bitten. These are then masked with a stopping-out varnish and the plate is re-immersed in the acid. This process can be repeated as many times as necessary. The most deeply bitten lines will hold most ink and therefore be the darkest areas of the final print.

INTAGLIO PRINTING

Etchings, engravings, aquatints and mezzotints are all intaglio printmaking processes and are printed in an identical way. It is quite different from the printing of wood-engravings, woodcuts and linocuts (all relief prints) where the printing ink is simply rolled onto the surface. With intaglio the ink fills all the lines which have been incised in the plate and the surface is wiped clean.

The plate is cleaned of all ground, stopping-out varnishes etc. Ink is thoroughly worked into the warmed plate so that it penetrates all of the lines. The surface of the plate is then cleaned with muslin pads taking great care not to drag ink out of the lines. This is laborious and skilled work. The inked plate is placed face-up on the flat bed of the press, a sheet of dampened paper is placed on it and blankets laid on top. The press is rather like a clothes mangle, and when the wheel is turned the bed passes between two rollers. The extreme pressure exerted by the press forces the softened paper into the lines on the plate and drags out the ink. The lines on intaglio prints are thus slightly raised from the surface of the paper.

The plate has to be re-inked for every impression. Repeated printing wears the plate; drypoints in particular will deteriorate quickly, and an early impression will be much superior to a later one.

LINE-ENGRAVING
An engraver uses a tool called a burin or graver to cut directly into the metal with a pushing action. A V-shaped groove is incised into the plate and the curls of metal thrown up along its path are scraped away. These sharply defined lines give a more brilliant effect than etched lines. Engraving demands great skill and etching is the easiest intaglio method for an amateur to try. A burin is sometimes used to strengthen areas of an etched plate.

MEZZOTINT
Mezzotint is an intaglio process that does not involve the use of acid. The copper plate is 'grounded' with a serrated tool known as a mezzotint rocker. This tool is 'rocked' over the plate in numerous directions leaving tiny pits where the serrations are pressed into the metal. If a print is pulled from this roughened plate it will be a rich, even black over its entire surface. The artist then works from dark to light and uses scrapers and burnishers to smooth the areas he wishes to print as lighter tones. It is a laborious process that was formerly much used for reproducing oil paintings because of the full range of tones that can be achieved. As with drypoint, the mezzotint burr is fragile and the plate wears quickly during the printing process.

PLATE-MARK
The enormous pressure exerted by a printing press gives intaglio prints one of the most distinguishing features of the process, the plate-mark. This is the indented line made by the perimeter of the plate as it is pressed into the paper during printing.

SOFT-GROUND ETCHING
The usual etching ground is hard enough to be freely handled and elastic enough to permit the needle to be moved freely across it. Soft-ground sticks to whatever touches it. A sheet of paper is laid onto the grounded plate and the drawing made into the paper. The pressure of the drawing implement makes the soft wax ground adhere to the underside of the paper. When the paper is peeled off the wax corresponding to the drawn lines is removed with it and the metal exposed ready for biting. The finished print closely resembles a chalk or pencil drawing.

SURFACE TONE
Tone created by leaving films of ink on the plate during the wiping.

SELECTED BIBLIOGRAPHY

Unless otherwise stated, the place of publication is London.

Anderson, Stanley, correspondence with Alvin Rolfs, 1944-1964, copies in City of Bristol Museum & Art Gallery, Dept. of Fine Art.

Barclay, Celia, *The Ugly Merman – Nathaniel Sparks, R.E., His Life and Family*, unpublished MS, 1989, copy in City of Bristol Museum & Art Gallery, Dept. of Fine Art.

Broome, Cecil W, [*Biographical sketches of Artist Members of Bristol Savages 1904-1977*], untitled typescript, n.d., copy in City of Bristol Museum & Art Gallery, Dept. of Fine Art.

Catalogue of Etchings, Engravings & Colour Prints, Frost & Reed Ltd., Bristol and London, 1925, p. 130-137 [Woollard].

Cox, Warren E (ed.), *The Homelovers Book, Etchings, Engravings and Colour Prints for Home Decoration*, Frost & Reed Ltd., Bristol and London. 24th ed., 1939, p. 137, 160, 176-7, 185 [Woollard].

Exhibition catalogues: Bristol Savages, Chicago Society of Etchers, Royal Society of Painter-Etchers and Engravers, Royal West of England Academy.

Graves, Algernon, *The Royal Academy Exhibitors 1760-1904*, 1905.

Gray, Basil, *The English Print*, 1937.

Griffiths, Anthony, *Prints and Printmaking. An Introduction to the history and techniques*, British Museum Publications Ltd., 1980.

Grouse: The Bristol Savages Magazine, 1921-1934.

Guichard, Kenneth M, *British Etchers 1850-1940*, 2nd ed., 1981.

Hamilton-Smith, George, *Catalogue of Etchings: relating to the City of Bristol and its immediate neighbourhood, 1862-1913*, privately printed, 1913.

Hardie, Martin, 'The Etchings and Engravings of Stanley Anderson', *Print Collector's Quarterly*, Vol. 20, 1933, p. 221-246.

Holme, Charles (ed.), *Modern Etching and Engraving*, (The Studio, Special Summer Number) 1902, pl. 13-14 [Bush].

Holme, Charles (ed.), *Modern Etchings, Mezzotints and Dry-Points*, (The Studio, Special Number) 1913, p. 19-20 [Bush].

Hubbard, E Hesketh (ed.), *66 Etchings*, Breamore (Print Society Publications No. 2) 1923, pl. 72-73 [Woollard].

Laver, James, *A History of British and American Etching*, 1929 [Full bibliography].

Lumsden, E S, *The Art of Etching*, 1924.

Potter, David and Sue, *Harry Banks 1869-1947*, MS biography, c. 1983, copy in City of Bristol Museum & Art Gallery, Dept. of Fine Art.

Royal Academy Exhibitors 1905-1970, Wakefield, 1973.

Salaman, Malcolm C, *Malcolm Osborne R.A., R.E.: Modern Masters of Etching No. 21*, 1929.

Salaman, Malcolm C (ed.), *Fine Prints of the Year*, 1923-1938.

Salaman, Malcolm C, 'The Royal College of Art Engraving School', *The Studio*, Vol. LII, 1929, p. 280-290.

Stewart-Wilson, Mary, *Queen Mary's Dolls' House*, 1988.

Tanner, Robin, *The Etcher's Craft*, Bristol, 1980.

Waite, Colston, *The Story of the Bristol Savages*, privately printed, Bristol, 1971.

Wedmore, Frederick, 'Recent Etching and Engraving', *The Studio*, Vol. XXIII, 1901, p. 14-22 [Bush].

Who's Who in Art, 3rd ed. 1934; 4th ed. 1948; 9th ed. 1958.

Woollard, Dorothy, correspondence with Herbert Bolton, 1922-4, City of Bristol Museum & Art Gallery, historical file 855.